ONE-MINUTE
Insights

Charisma
HOUSE
A STRANG COMPANY

Most STRANG COMMUNICATIONS BOOK GROUP products are available at special quantity discounts for bulk purchase for sales promotions, premiums, fund-raising, and educational needs. For details, write Strang Communications Book Group, 600 Rinehart Road, Lake Mary, Florida 32746, or telephone (407) 333-0600.

ONE-MINUTE INSIGHTS edited by Charisma House
Published by Charisma House
A Strang Company
600 Rinehart Road
Lake Mary, Florida 32746
www.strangbookgroup.com

Unless otherwise noted, all Scripture quotations are from the New King James Version of the Bible. Copyright © 1979, 1980, 1982 by Thomas Nelson, Inc., publishers. Used by permission.

Scripture quotations marked AMP are from the Amplified Bible. Old Testament copyright © 1965, 1987 by the Zondervan Corporation. The Amplified New Testament copyright © 1954, 1958, 1987 by the Lockman Foundation. Used by permission.

Scripture quotations marked KJV are from the King James Version of the Bible.

Scripture quotations marked NAS are from the New American Standard Bible, copyright © 1960, 1962, 1963, 1968, 1971, 1972, 1973, 1975, 1977, 1995 by The Lockman Foundation. Used by permission. (www.Lockman.org)

Scripture quotations marked NIV are from the Holy Bible, New International Version. Copyright © 1973, 1978, 1984, International Bible Society. Used by permission.

Scripture quotations marked NLT are from the Holy Bible, New Living Translation, copyright © 1996, 2004. Used by permission of Tyndale House Publishers, Inc., Wheaton, IL 60189. All rights reserved.

Cover design by Bill Johnson

Copyright © 2010 by Charisma House
All rights reserved

Library of Congress Cataloging-in-Publication Data:

One-minute insights / edited by Charisma House.
    p. cm.
  Includes bibliographical references (p.   ).
  ISBN 978-1-61638-150-9
  1. Christian life--Meditations. I. Charisma House. II. Title.
  BV4501.3.O54 2010
  242--dc22

                    2010008592

10 11 12 13 14 — 9 8 7 6 5 4 3 2 1
Printed in the United States of America

CONTENTS

Introduction: Fresh Insights for

Standing Strong.. 1

1   Forgiveness *versus* Unforgiveness 4

2   Faith *versus* Fear 8

3   Life's Opportunities *versus*

Life's Challenges...12

4   Spirit Possession *versus*

Demonic Oppression 16

5   Spiritual Cleansing *versus*

Sinful Uncleanness...20

ONE-MINUTE INSIGHTS

6 The Power of Prophecy *versus*

   the Power of the Tongue.............................24

7 Reconciliation *versus* Offense.............................28

8 Heaven *versus* Hell.............................32

9 Covenant for Healing *versus*

   Hindrances to Healing.............................36

10 The Mountain of God *versus*

    the Cave of Withdrawal.............................40

11 True Prophecy *versus* False Prophecy.............................44

12 The Armor of God *versus*

    the Wiles of the Enemy.............................48

13 God's Unmerited Favor *versus*

Sin's Condemnation 52

14 The Blessed Man *versus* the Cursed Man.............56

15 Unity *versus* Conflict...60

16 God's Timing *versus* Man's Timing 64

17 Heavenly Angels *versus* Fallen Angels.....................68

18 The Battlefield of the Mind *versus*

Your Enemy Opponent 72

19 Alone *versus* Loneliness.......................................76

20 Answered Prayer *versus*

Unanswered Prayer...80

ONE-MINUTE INSIGHTS

21 What Love Is *versus* What Love Is Not................84

22 The Fear of God *versus* Afraid of God..................88

23 Fasting for Breakthrough *versus*

    King Stomach's Reign..92

24 Rebuilt by the Holy Spirit *versus*

    Broken-Down Walls of Sin...............................96

25 Facing Tomorrow With Joy *versus*

    Facing Tomorrow With Fear.................................100

    Notes 105

Introduction

FRESH INSIGHTS
FOR STANDING STRONG

THE WORLD IS in a precarious situation—economically, morally, politically, and spiritually. When you turn on the evening news, read the morning newspaper, or discuss things with your acquaintances and friends, before long you will get the message that things have never quite been as bad as they are right now. The more we attempt to analyze and solve the issues of our day, the more the equations seem to add up to hopelessness.[1]

But this book is not about the world—it's about you, the person who lives in today's world and is trying to make sense of what is going on in your own life. It is filled with twenty-five insights that will help you to live principled in a world where anything goes.

This book has been developed to help you to find answers to some of the issues you may be facing—and to do it in one-minute segments. For example, do you find it difficult to forgive others (or yourself) for wrongs that happened

and that hurt you deeply? The first chapter of this book, "Forgiveness *versus* Unforgiveness," will provide you with some principles for learning to forgive and challenge you with the blessings of forgiveness.

Do you struggle with loneliness? Do you feel alone even in the midst of a crowd—or while sitting in your living room with family members? Turn to chapter 19 to find some insights about the contrast between *being alone* and *dealing with loneliness*.

Or has the precarious condition of our world threatened you to the point of being afraid to face the future? Don't stop reading until you reach chapter 25, where you will discover the difference between facing tomorrow with joy and facing tomorrow with fear.

When you feel overwhelmed by the circumstances of life, ask the Holy Spirit to show you what *He is doing in your life*. He wants to get your attention. He will bring the power of the cleansing blood of Jesus that not only carries away the stains of sin but also filters out whatever is toxic to His new life.[2]

He is your permanent Helper. He has come to help you see your life rebuilt and advanced into His purposes. He will respond to your every prayer, and He will establish, strengthen, and settle you, today and every day for the rest of your life.[3]

So stop what you are doing right now, take a minute, and get some fresh insight from God to help you to stand strong no matter what is going on in your world.

—CHARISMA HOUSE EDITORS

Forgiveness

*Sincerely asking God to let those who have
hurt us off the hook*

TOTAL FORGIVENESS IS a choice. It is not a feeling—at least at first—but is rather an act of the will. It is the choice to tear up the record of wrongs we have been keeping. When we develop a lifestyle of total forgiveness, we learn to erase the wrong rather than file it away in our mental computer.

Total forgiveness must take place in the heart. Confidence toward God is ultimately what total forgiveness is all about; He is the One I want to please at the end of the day. He cares and knows whether I have truly and totally forgiven, and when I *know* I have His love and approval, I am one very happy and contented servant of Christ.[4]

Unforgiveness

*Living with bitterness, anger, and self-pity because of
what another did to hurt us*

BITTERNESS AND UNFORGIVENESS demonstrate an inward condition. It is an excessive desire for vengeance that comes from deep resentment. It heads the list of things that grieve the Spirit of God. It is one of the most frequent causes of people missing the grace of God.

This inward condition of unforgiveness will manifest itself in many ways—losing your temper, high blood pressure, irritability, sleeplessness, obsession with getting even, depression, isolation, a constant negative perspective, and generally feeling unwell.

We must, therefore, begin to get rid of a bitter and unforgiving spirit; otherwise, the attempt to forgive will fail.[5]

Forgiveness

Ask Yourself

Do I have resentment or bitterness in my heart because of something someone did to me or said about me? Do I lack inner peace?

Relinquishing bitterness is an open invitation for the Holy Spirit to give you His peace, His joy, and the knowledge of His will.

Remember

But if you do not forgive men their sins, your Father will not forgive your sins.

—MATTHEW 6:15, NIV

Unforgiveness

Ask Yourself

Are you praying for God's blessings to rain on the lives of your offenders? Why not?

The desire to punish another is the opposite of perfect love and total forgiveness.

Remember

Bear with each other and forgive whatever grievances you may have against one another.
—COLOSSIANS 3:13, NIV

Faith

Identifying and defeating the source of fear in your life by using God's fear fighters

I‍T IS NOT God's will for your life to be ruled by fear—of any kind. Yet fear is one of the greatest evils you must face off with—and win! So, to live a victorious life, you need to take the challenge personally to become a fear fighter. Your faith will overcome your fear when you determine to become a fear fighter.

To be an effective fear fighter, you will need God's arsenal of divine weapons—His fear fighters. Declare His Word in faith, and nothing life throws at you will overwhelm you, defeat you, or cause you to live in fear.[6]

Fear

Wasting energy and emotion fearing things that may never materialize

FEAR IS NOT rational. It is not based on fact. Researchers have found that 40 percent of the things we worry about *never* happen. Only 8 percent of things we worry about are even *likely* to happen.[7]

Fear and worry work to deceive you by appearances. How much energy and emotion have you wasted over things that never materialized? We lie awake at night thinking that this bad thing is going to happen…yet it never does. It is simply much ado about nothing. Instead of cringing in fear, begin to declare, "Jesus is with me. I refuse to make much ado about nothing."[8]

Faith

Ask Yourself

How are you exercising your faith to believe God? How can God's power, love, and gift of a sound mind help you overcome your fears?

When fear threatens your victory, preach three simple truths about faith: Faith is important. It doesn't take huge faith. I have faith for this.

Remember

As soon as Jesus heard the word that was spoken, He said to the ruler of the synagogue, "Do not be afraid; only believe."

—MARK 5:36

Fear

Ask Yourself

What do you fear most in life? Illness? Job loss? Failure? Your children's welfare?

Fear is one of the greatest evils you must face off with—and win!

Remember

For God has not given us a spirit of fear, but of power and of love and of a sound mind.

—2 TIMOTHY 1:7

Life's Opportunities

*Using God's custom-designed promises to journey
through the problems of life and receive the supernatural
provision available*

IT IS IMPERATIVE for God's children to discover the principle for transforming the problems of our lives into the provisions of God. Promise, problem, and provision are a supernatural principle based on the Word of God. A problem is an opportunity to step into a new dimension of accomplishment.

Do you need a miracle? When you want what you've never had, you need to do what you've never done. You need to have faith in God, because nothing is impossible to those who believe in a God who never fails. Faith is the victory that overcomes the world.[9]

Life's Challenges

*Recognizing the warning sign that something
is not quite right*

PROBLEMS HAPPEN TO every member of the human race. Albert Einstein once said, "The only reason for time is so that everything doesn't happen at once." Thank God! Most of us can handle only one problem at a time; however, problems usually do come in pairs. They make no appointments; they do not respect age, nationality, or levels of income; and they usually stay in your life much longer than you want them to.

Challenges and problems don't prevent you from reaching your destiny—you do. God has painted a portrait of your life. He knows every detail of your future. The tests, trials, and tribulations of your life are purposed by God so that you may achieve your divine potential.[10]

Life's Opportunities

Ask Yourself

Are you proclaiming God's promises in faith?

Your vision for your life determines God's provision in your life!

Remember

Your Father knows what you need before you ask Him.

—MATTHEW 6:8, NAS

Life's Challenges

Ask Yourself

Do you trust God to take you through the problem and into your provision?

Your success in life is ultimately measured by the problems you create—or solve.

Remember

Many are the afflictions of the righteous, but the LORD delivers him out of them all.

—PSALM 34:19

Spirit Possession

*Breaking the oppressing power of the enemy through the
possessing power of the Holy Spirit*

POSSESSION IMPLIES OWNERSHIP. We are owned
by the Lord Jesus! We are purchased, redeemed, and
bought with a price. We are possessed by the Holy Spirit of
God, who lives in our spirit. Oppression takes place in the
soul and in the flesh.

Allow the Holy Spirit to control your life—all of you, all
the time. Allow the Holy Spirit to have His way with you.
Pray throughout the day. Let the Holy Spirit show you negative attitudes, habits, feelings, and behavior that need to be
changed. The Holy Spirit is God's power given in order for
you to become like Jesus Christ. He will show you things
through the Bible, other people, and your experience.[11]

Demonic Oppression

Sweeping clean the demonic influences impacting your life and the lives of others

YOU MAY BE just like many others who question deliverance. Perhaps you have asked the question, "But I am a Christian. How can I have demons?" The presence of the Holy Spirit does not prevent evil spirits from dwelling in a believer's body or soul. Believers are targets for demon powers, but demons cannot enter a person by choice. There must be a "gate" or doorway of opportunity. If gates are kept closed, the enemy cannot gain access!

Like reading, 'riting, and 'rithmatic, there are *three Rs* for walking in liberty from demonic oppression that have been given by the Lord Jesus Christ: *Recognize* the enemy and their plan of attack. *Resist*—Satan is a thief, and a thief must be resisted! *Remain* in the Lord—rest in Him, abide in Him, and relax in the promises of God.[12]

Spirit Possession

Ask Yourself

Have you welcomed the Holy Spirit into your life? Are you Holy Spirit possessed?

It is our spirit that is born again, and it is in our spirit that the Holy Spirit of God takes up residence.

Remember

Behold, I give unto you power…over all the power of the enemy.

—LUKE 10:19, KJV

Demonic Oppression

Ask Yourself

Could demons be the source of *your* struggles?

When we bind demons in the name of Jesus Christ, we speak it and God honors it.

Remember

Many are the afflictions of the righteous, but the LORD delivers him out of them all.

—PSALM 34:19

Spiritual Cleansing

Stepping deeply into the Lord's presence so He can reveal areas in our hearts that need to be cleansed

WITHIN THE HEART of every Christian there is a secret place, a sanctuary we must prepare for the Lord. Not until this place is cleansed will the Lord dwell within us in the fullness of His Spirit; not until this room is pure will we truly become a house for the Lord.

Our goal is not merely to be "good" but to see God and, in seeing Him, to do what He does. We can be assured that each step deeper into the Lord's presence will reveal areas in our hearts that need to be cleansed. Do not be afraid. When the Spirit shows you areas of sin, it is not to condemn you but to cleanse you. If we will gain God's greatest blessings, we must embrace His highest purpose.[13]

Sinful Uncleanness

Recognizing those secret things that defile the temple of God within

IN 2 CHRONICLES 29, King Hezekiah commanded the priests to carry the uncleanness out from the holy place. The call to clean the holy place was not an option; it was a command. The priests entered the holy place and brought out the unclean things.

In the new covenant temple, the church, it is our private, inner lives that need this deep cleansing. We have inherited traditions that justify and reinforce darkness of soul within us. Most Christians have little hope that purity of heart is even attainable. The revival that will turn a nation begins in the trembling unveiling of our hearts, in the removal of what is defiled and hidden within us. I will tell you a mystery. It is in this very place, this chamber of our deepest secrets, that the door to eternity is found.[14]

Spiritual Cleansing

Ask Yourself

Is the door of your heart opened toward God? Are you willing for His penetrating, cleansing work?

Not until we are cleansed of sin will God's purposes for us become clear. Indeed, it is the pure in heart who see God.

Remember

They…went in to cleanse the house of the LORD, according to the commandment of the king by the words of the LORD.

—2 CHRONICLES 29:15, NAS

Sinful Uncleanness

Ask Yourself

Have you renounced the hidden sins of your heart in order to receive God's holiness?

To ascend the hill of the Lord, to stand in the holy place, we must have clean hands and a pure heart.

Remember

Who may ascend into the hill of the LORD? And who may stand in His holy place? He who has clean hands and a pure heart.

—PSALM 24:3–4, NAS

The Power of Prophecy

Speaking by the inspiration of the Holy Spirit

SPIRIT-FILLED BELIEVERS TODAY can also speak by the inspiration of the Holy Spirit. Those who experience the manifestation of tongues can also prophesy. The Holy Spirit will inspire the believer to do both. The key is yielding to the Holy Spirit and allowing Him to inspire you to speak not only in a tongue that you do not comprehend and have not learned but also in your native language.

We believers can also pray, sing, teach, and preach by the inspiration of the Spirit. All results of the Holy Spirit's inspiration are different types of prophetic manifestations in action. We should welcome and cultivate all forms of the Spirit's inspiration.[15]

The Power of the Tongue

Mastering the what, when, and why
of the words you speak

THE FACT THAT we are not perfect and are not expected to be perfect is no warrant from God to settle for imperfection. Some of the great people in biblical history—Abraham, David, or John, for example—were not perfect. The imperfection was almost always traceable to the tongue.

We therefore have a mandate to deal with our tongues. We should have a desire that goes from the crown of our heads to the soles of our feet and to our fingertips to please God. Therefore we should want to pursue control of the tongue while accepting that we will only make measured, or limited, progress. But knowing that this pursuit truly pleases God is good enough for me![16]

ONE-MINUTE INSIGHTS

The Power of Prophecy

Ask Yourself

Are you willing to allow the Holy Spirit to speak through you?

The Holy Spirit will inspire a person, but He will not force someone to speak. People can decide whether or not to utter an inspired message.

Remember

Quench not the Spirit. Despise not prophesyings.
—1 THESSALONIANS 5:19–20, KJV

The Power of the Tongue

Ask Yourself

Before you speak, do you ask yourself, "Are the words I'm about to say necessary? Are they harmless or hurtful?"

Tongue control is a noble goal: it leads to self-discipline in every area of our lives.

Remember

Men will have to give account on the day of judgment for every careless word they have spoken.

—MATTHEW 12:36, NIV

Reconciliation

*Maintaining a bond of peace through an attitude of
humility, gentleness, and long-suffering*

THE WORD OF reconciliation begins on the common
ground that we have all sinned against God. We do
not desire reconciliation or salvation unless we know there
is a separation. Since we are to imitate God (see Ephesians
5:1), we are to extend reconciliation to a brother who sins
against us. Jesus established this pattern: go to him and show
him his sin, not to condemn him but to remove anything
that lies between the two of you, and thus be reconciled
and restored. The goodness of God within us will draw our
brother to repentance and restoration of the relationship.

If we keep the love of God as our motivation, we will not
fail. Love never fails. When we love others the way Jesus
loves us, we will be free even if the other person chooses not
to be reconciled to us.[17]

Offense

*Beginning a progression from offense to betrayal
and from betrayal to hatred*

SATAN IS SUBTLE and delights in deception. He is shrewd in his operations, cunning and crafty. Don't forget he can disguise himself as a messenger of light.

One of his most deceptive and insidious kinds of bait is something every Christian has encountered—offense. Offended people produce much fruit, such as hurt, anger, outrage, jealousy, resentment, strife, bitterness, hatred, and envy. Some of the consequences of picking up an offense are insults, attacks, wounding, division, separation, broken relationships, betrayal, and backsliding.

Freedom from offense is essential for every Christian because Jesus said it is impossible to live this life and not have the opportunity to be offended (Luke 17:1).[18]

Reconciliation

Ask Yourself

Are you willing to selflessly lay down your life to walk in godly love—even when offended?

The love of God is the key to freedom from the baited trap of offense.

Remember

If it is possible, as much as depends on you, live peaceably with all men.

—ROMANS 12:18

Offense

Ask Yourself

Have you forgotten the command of God to live by the laws of love?

A betrayal in the kingdom of God comes when a believer seeks his own benefit or protection at the expense of another believer.

Remember

And then many will be offended, will betray one another, and will hate one another.
—MATTHEW 24:10

Heaven

*Experiencing the miracle of the presence of the Lord in
His heavenly home*

WORDS CAN'T DESCRIBE the range of emotions I experienced in the presence of the Lord. Just a moment before, I had been in the bowels of hell, just like someone who didn't know Jesus, and was cursed and damned to eternal torment.

Peace had replaced terror, and safety took the place of danger. The feelings of worthlessness, shame, and humiliation disappeared as the value that He had placed on me was revealed. It was then that I truly understood how much God loves us. I was at once comforted, protected, and completely relieved. I just wanted to remain at His feet. I was so grateful that I did know Jesus, that I was a Christian. I just wanted to worship Him.[19]

Hell

Landing in the horrors of everlasting torment, fear, thirst,
isolation, and hopelessness in the pit of fire

I FOUND MYSELF NEXT to an enormous pit with raging flames of fire leaping high into an open cavern. As I looked up into that dark, eerie, tomb-like atmosphere, it seemed to be a mouth that had swallowed her dead. The flames of her ravenous appetite were never satisfied with the pitiful screams of untold multitudes.

I could see the outlines of people through the flames. The screams from the condemned souls were deafening and relentless. There was no safe place, no safe moment, no temporary relief of any kind. In hell, the state of fear never ceases for even one second. It lasts for an eternity. There is no way of escape. No one can rescue you.[20]

Heaven

Ask Yourself

Have you chosen eternal life with God or eternal death with Satan?

"I understood that it was out of His great love for mankind that He wanted them to know this place [heaven] exists, so they could instead choose life with Him."

Remember

He who has the Son has life; he who does not have the Son of God does not have life.

—1 JOHN 5:12

Hell

Ask Yourself

Have you accepted the only provision that will keep you out of hell—God's salvation?

"You may wonder how a good and loving God could send someone to that horrific place called hell. He doesn't. It is your rejection of the provision [Jesus] for your sin that sends you there."

Remember

I have set before you life and death, blessing and cursing; therefore *choose life.*
> —DEUTERONOMY 30:19, EMPHASIS ADDED

Covenant for Healing

Finding healing through God's healing covenant

WHEN GOD FIRST established His covenant with man, He also became man's great provider. This included provision of spiritual, financial, emotional, and physical needs—even physical healing. In Exodus 15:26, God introduced Himself as Israel's healer and called Himself *Jehovah Rapha*. The Hebrew word *rapha* alludes to stitching something that has been torn or completely repairing something that needs to be mended. Figuratively, it means to cure someone.

Through His healing covenant God declared, "If you will obey My Word and walk in My commandments, I will prevent disease from coming upon you." In the time of Christ, He instructed His followers to ask the heavenly Father in His name, and He would do it (John 16:23). Throughout Christ's ministry, He not only gave a message of hope and salvation, but He also combined the message of eternal salvation with healing of the mind and body.[21]

Hindrances to Healing

Losing out on healing because of a lack of communication with God (prayer)—the verbal umbilical cord that connects us to God

HAVE YOU EVER prayed and felt that the ceiling of the church was a sheet of brass? Has your worship ever felt as though you are speaking into a hollowed log? Or have you ever prayed for a specific need to be met and felt like your words were lost in outer space? If prayers can be hindered, then so can the manifestation of your healing.

All new covenant blessings are based upon an active relationship with Christ, not a mental knowledge of God or an intellectual understanding of certain spiritual concepts, but an inner working of the Holy Spirit that comes through confessing Christ as your Savior and Lord. Some people receive Christ as Savior because they want fire insurance (they want to escape hell), but a true covenant believer will also accept Christ's lordship, meaning He is the master—the boss, if you please—and you are His obedient servant.[22]

Covenant for Healing

Ask Yourself

Why is the knowledge of God's healing covenant important to you?

There is no such thing as a day of miracles or a day of healing; there is only a covenant of healing established by God.

Remember

Bless the LORD, O my soul, and forget now all his benefits: Who forgiveth all thine iniquities, who healeth all thy diseases.

—PSALM 103:2–3, KJV

Hindrances to Healing

Ask Yourself

If your prayers for healing seem to be hitting a ceiling of brass, have you made certain of your relationship with Jesus?

If believers persist in housing an unforgiving spirit in their hearts, Scripture gives strong repercussions that will follow. Understanding this reveals how unforgiveness is the greatest hindrance to receiving healing.

Remember

Confess your trespasses [faults] to one another, and pray for one another, that you may be healed.

—JAMES 5:16

The Mountain of God

Becoming inwardly repelled by the superficial distractions
of modern Christianity and desperate for more of God

HOREB WAS "THE mountain of God." At Horeb we not only discover more about God but also finally begin to understand ourselves and what the Lord desires of us. Our lives simplify and truly focus on that which is most important.

Beloved, you know you are at Horeb when God cuts you back to the root source of your spiritual life. Yes, you are at Horeb when you are inwardly repelled by the superficial distractions of modern Christianity and desperate for more of God.

For those who are even now at Horeb, I urge you to let your soul open and your pain rise to God. He knows. He sees your heartache. He feels your sense of shame, bewilderment, and regret. Whatever He says, do it. When you leave Horeb, He will have brought you to a level you previously thought unattainable.[23]

The Cave of Withdrawal

Withdrawing into the spiritual cave of self-pity and isolation from God

E LIJAH, STRESSED AND discouraged, withdrew into a cave on Horeb. For us, self-pity can also become a spiritual cave. It can trap us in a dark hole of loneliness and pain. In this place of isolation we fail to hear the encouragement of God. All we really hear is the echo of our own voice magnifying and distorting our problems.

We must learn to detect, without great signs, the still, small voice of God. He will not fight for our attention; He must be sought. He will not startle us; He must be perceived. It took no special skill to "discern" the earthquake, the fire, or the great storm, but to sense the holy quiet of God, our other activities must cease. In our world of great pressures and continual distractions, the attention of our hearts must rise to the invisible world of God's Spirit. We must learn to see Him who is unseen.[24]

The Mountain of God

Ask Yourself

Are you ready to walk with God through a Horeb experience?

At Horeb the morphine of religion wears off, and we can once again feel our pain. Reality manifests. We see ourselves in the light of God, and as we do, we fall upon Christ the cornerstone (Luke 20:18). Though "broken to pieces," we are finally fit to be used by God.

Remember

Now Moses was tending the flock of Jethro his father-in-law, the priest of Midian. And he led the flock to the back of the desert, and came to Horeb, the mountain of God.

—EXODUS 3:1

The Cave of Withdrawal

Ask Yourself

When you are hidden away from the chaos of the world, are you listening closely for the still small voice of God?

We must learn to recognize the nearness of the Lord when there are no "earthquakes" or "storms" to capture our attention. He demands we enter a more refined relationship with Him, one that is based on His love and the whisper of His Word, not merely on spiritual phenomena or the issues of our times.

Remember

And behold, the LORD passed by...but the LORD was not in the wind; and...the LORD was not in the earthquake; and...the LORD was not in the fire; and after the fire a still small voice.
—1 KINGS 19:11–12

True Prophecy

Recognizing that prophets are to be ordained and sent under proper, godly authority

SCRIPTURE GIVES US a clear definition of a true prophet. The word *prophet* in the Old Testament Hebrew is *nabiy*, which is simply a man inspired of God. A female is referred to as a *prophetess*, which is *nebiyah*, or a woman inspired of God. Any Christian can receive divine inspiration, but a prophet is unique because his inspiration is designed specifically for speaking out and communicating a special message from God.

Your personality has little to do with your type of calling. Your personality only makes your calling special and unique. Prophets, according to the Bible, are those who are called of God to stand in a spiritual office and be God's divinely inspired spokespeople. To say it even more simply: *the man or woman called specifically to be a messenger from God speaks under the divine inspiration of God.*[25]

False Prophecy

Failing to strive for the highest level of accuracy in receiving and delivering the secrets of God

HOW DO WE recognize a false prophet today? Jesus mentioned that we would know them by their fruits. Second Peter 2:1–18 gives us a list of the fruits or characteristics of a false prophet. These verses identify the fruit of false prophets. We must be able to measure the message of every prophet against the Bible.

Don't purposely use your gift to sin as the false prophet does, but if you make a mistake, don't condemn yourself; God's grace will cover you. The apostle Paul had shortcomings and made mistakes. But his motive, purpose, and daily quest were to do right in serving God. There is grace for you to step out and try in the prophetic. The key is to stay pure and submitted to others. As you learn to walk in God's anointing, you will stand with those who reveal the true secrets of the Lord.[26]

True Prophecy

Ask Yourself

Since God did give some prophets, then we need to make room for them. Who are we to say we don't need them when God gave them?

Prophets are anointed vessels that God has set into the church, not to be a problem, but as a wonderful blessing.

Remember

And He Himself gave...some prophets.
—EPHESIANS 4:11

False Prophecy

Ask Yourself

Have you learned to measure the message of every prophet against the Word of God?

We simply cannot label someone a false prophet based on whether his prophecies are accurate.

Remember

Now our knowledge is partial and incomplete, and even the gift of prophecy reveals only part of the whole picture!

—1 CORINTHIANS 13:9, NLT

The Armor of God

Preparing to engage the enemy (Satan) in battle and come out victoriously

THE ARMOR OF God is not for special or set-apart saints for spiritual warfare. It is not for fivefold ministry gifts. Ephesians 6:10 says, "Finally my brethren, be strong in the Lord and in the power of His might." The verse indicates that the armor of God is for "the brethren." This means it is simply for those who are saved and blood bought. Every person in the body of Christ should be putting on the whole armor of God!

The significance of the whole armor of God is that no part works alone. If you have your feet shod with peace and do not have on the helmet of salvation, it is futile. Every piece of the armor has been given to us by God to wear in evil days.[27]

The Wiles of the Enemy

Understanding that Satan is subtly waiting to snare believers into worshiping him instead of worshiping God

THE HEBREW WORD for *wiles* is *nekel*. It means "treachery, conspiracy, beguilement, subtle, deceit, trickery, and deception." To be subject to the wiles of the enemy means to be deceived. Few people willingly worship the devil. His methods blind their minds into making them think they are doing anything but worshiping. Worship is what warfare is all about—God desires our worship, but the devil wants to be worshiped as well.

When we accept the things of the world from the devil, it is the highest form of worship. Worship is not just *what we do* but *what we abstain from doing!*[28]

The Armor of God

Ask Yourself

Are you spiritually dressed (head to toe) in the armor of God and ready to go forth equipped for battle?

The foundational purpose for the armor of God is to give us the power to stand against the wiles of the enemy in the midst of evil days.

Remember

Put on the whole armor of God, that you may be able to stand against the wiles of the devil.
—EPHESIANS 6:11

The Wiles of the Enemy

Ask Yourself

Have you fallen prey to Satan's subtle attacks by letting down your spiritual defenses?

Here's the foundational truth of the wiles of the devil: to lie behind the scenes and watch a person until a vulnerable moment arises so that he can attack.

Remember

I will put enmity between you and the woman…and her Offspring…you will lie in wait and bruise his heel.

—GENESIS 3:15, AMP

God's Unmerited Favor

Experiencing the righteousness of Jesus through His unmerited favor

THERE IS NO doubt that all believers want to experience God's unmerited favor in their lives. All of us want to experience success in our marriages, families, and careers as well as ministries. We all want to enjoy God's best and richest blessings. We want His provision, health, and power flowing mightily in our lives, and we know that all these blessings are wrapped up in God's unmerited favor. When His unmerited favor is on your side, nothing can stand against you. But if His favor is unmerited, how can we qualify for it? If we cannot earn, deserve, or merit it, how can we be confident that we have His unmerited favor?

Your righteousness in Christ is the sure foundation on which you can build your expectations to receive God's unmerited favor. God sees you through the lens of the cross of His Son, and as Jesus is today deserving of blessings, peace, health, and favor, so are you![29]

Sin's Condemnation

*Allowing the enemy to use the law to heap condemnation
upon you, distancing you from God*

THE LAW WAS designed to show "all the world" that they are guilty of sin before God. NO flesh can be justified by the deeds of the Law. All humanity needs the Savior to rescue them! God gave the Law to expose man's sin!

The Law does not stop sin. It stirs up sin and produces "all manner of evil desire"! In other words, without the Law, there would be no knowledge of sin. You can drive at any speed that you like on a road that doesn't have a speed limit, and nobody can accuse you of speeding. But once the authorities put a speed limit on the same road, you now have the knowledge that if you drive beyond seventy miles an hour on this road, you would be breaking the law.

The enemy always pours accusations on you using the voice of a legalist. He uses the Law to show up your failures, to put a spotlight on how your behavior has disqualified you from fellowship with God, and to constantly point out how you are undeserving of His acceptance, love, and blessings![30]

God's Unmerited Favor

Ask Yourself

Have you fully understood that God's righteousness is your right to His unmerited favor?

There is no middle road. You are either righteous by God's unmerited favor, or you are trying to merit righteousness with your own works.

Remember

For He [God] made Him [Jesus Christ] who knew no sin to be sin for us, that we might become the righteousness of God in Him [Jesus Christ].

—2 CORINTHIANS 5:21

Sin's Condemnation

Ask Yourself

Have you felt the condemnation of the law due to your failure to live perfectly according to the standards of the Law?

The enemy knows that the more condemnation and guilt you experience, the more likely you are to feel alienated from God and to continue in that sin.

Remember

Therefore by the deeds of the law no flesh will be justified in His sight, for by the law is the knowledge of sin.

—ROMANS 3:20

The Blessed Man

Enjoying divine health, youthfulness, vibrancy, and dynamism

GOD'S WORD IS amazing. It paints a beautiful picture of the blessed man in Jeremiah 17:7–8. When you depend on and trust in the Lord, Jesus will cause you to be a picture of robust strength, vitality, and good success. When you are blessed, there will be no stress, fear, and panic attacks because the blessed man "will not be anxious in the year of drought." A year of drought speaks of a severe famine, and in our modern vernacular, it would be no different from the global financial meltdown, the subprime crisis, the collapse of global investment banks, the volatile stock markets, and rising inflation.

While it may be bad news for the world, the blessed man can remain at rest and not be anxious because God has promised that even in the midst of a crisis, he will not "cease from yielding fruit." How will this happen? It will happen because he puts his trust in the Lord![31]

The Cursed Man

Falling under the curses of the Law, which condemns you

JEREMIAH 17:5 IS amazingly clear on how you can be a cursed man. When a man "trusts in man" and not in the Lord, he becomes a cursed man. To trust in man also refers to someone putting confidence in his own good works and efforts, claiming to be "self-made," choosing to depend on himself and rejecting God's unmerited favor.

A man who "makes flesh his strength" is also cursed. When you see the word *flesh* in your Bible, it does not always refer to your physical body. You have to look at the context of the verse. In this context, "flesh" can be paraphrased as "self-effort." In other words, we can read this verse as "Cursed is the man who trusts in man and makes *self-effort* his strength."[32]

The Blessed Man

Ask Yourself

Are you Christ's? Do you belong to Jesus? Then that makes you an heir according to the promise.

Jesus wants you to experience His blessings in your life. God's blessings are part of our inheritance in the new covenant of grace, which Jesus died to give us.

Remember

Blessed is the man who trusts in the LORD, and whose hope is the LORD. For he shall be like a tree planted by the waters, which spreads out its roots by the river.

—JEREMIAH 17:7–8

The Cursed Man

Ask Yourself

Do you pride yourself on being a self-made man or woman? If so, you have fallen under the curse of the Law.

When a believer rejects God's grace and depends on his own works to be blessed, he falls back under the curse of the law.

Remember

Cursed is the man who trusts in man and makes flesh his strength, whose heart departs from the LORD. For he shall be like a shrub in the desert, and shall not see when good comes.

—JEREMIAH 17:5–6

Unity

Living in harmony and producing a sweet sound before the Lord

GOD WANTS US to have blessed, powerful lives, and He knows such a life is not possible until we live in peace. Peace binds us to the precious Holy Spirit. God's Spirit is a spirit of peace. Jesus is the Prince of Peace. Jesus gave us peace, but it will certainly slip away from us if we are not determined to hang on to it. God's Word tells us that if we want to live in harmony with each other, we must pursue peace and go after it.

It's not enough to simply desire peace. We must actually live in peace in all of our relationships: our relationship with God, our relationship with others, and even our relationship with ourselves. To live in harmony and unity we must make allowances for each other and overlook each other's mistakes and faults. We must be humble, loving, compassionate, and courteous. We must be willing to forgive quickly and frequently. We must not be easily offended and must bless others rather than curse them. We must be generous in mercy, and we must be long-suffering (patient).[33]

Conflict

Allowing strife and conflict to spread like an infection or a highly contagious disease, contaminating and defiling many

THE BIBLE HAS much to say about strife and contention (which are actually the same thing) and points to strife as the source of many other kinds of problems. Strife leads to resentment, rancor, bitterness, or hatred. Left unconfronted, it destroys and devastates. It causes trouble and brings torment to church members and to church leadership, hindering God's work and contaminating many.

If we fail to recognize and resist strife, it poisons our attitudes and begins to negatively affect all of our relationships—at school, work, home, and church. What's worse is that we often have no idea when the problems even started or what to do about them.

Strife does not have to destroy your life. If you desire to walk in victory, it's not too late. Learn to recognize the spirit of strife and confront it. Refuse to be fuel for it, so that you can claim the righteousness, peace, and joy that are rightfully yours as a child of God.[34]

Unity

Ask Yourself

Do you have a present relationship in which you should attempt to pursue peace?

We were created to live in the love and excitement of harmonious relationships, free from dissension, confusion, and hurt.

Remember

Therefore let us pursue the things which make for peace and the things by which one may edify another.

—ROMANS 14:19

Conflict

Ask Yourself

Are you allowing conflict to negatively affect your relationships rather than resisting conflict when you become aware of it?

If you must strive at something, strive to keep strife and conflict out. Be diligent.

Remember

I myself always strive to have a conscience without offense toward God and men.

—ACTS 24:16

63

God's Timing

*Releasing the realignment of heaven and earth, which
moves you from conformity to transformation*

IMAGINE FOR A moment that all of eternity is repre-
sented by a large piece of paper. This is where God
is—unlimited by time and space. Now draw a line on that
piece of paper that represents time with a beginning and an
end. This line begins when God instituted time at Creation
and ends when God says, "Time's up."

We are living in a time when the will of heaven is being
communicated to God's prophets and apostles of this age.
This is releasing an *overpowering* strength in His people. Our
time and days are being *reordered*. We are learning to worship
and watch in new ways. When we move with God to watch
and pray, He reorders our day. When we are at the right place
at the right time, then we are assured of success and victory.

When the revelation of heaven confronts your mind with
truth and revelation, do not hesitate to embrace change.
Fear not because of your past! Your past will submit to
your future! Time cannot hold you captured in the past—
the best is still ahead for you.[35]

Man's Timing

*Breaking from any old cycle that has held your promise
and destiny in captivity*

ISRAEL FIRST HAD to complete the four hundred years
that were decreed by the Lord for the Israelites' captivity
in Egypt. Sometimes we are destined to wait until God's
perfect time of release. When we miss one opportunity, the
Lord brings us full circle to offer us the best again.

We do not want to repeat our wanderings and go through
the same cycle again. Old cycles can hang on for years, even
generations. Satan loves to keep those cycles in operation
from generation to generation in our lives.

Make a list of old cycles. Declare that your Passover time
of deliverance is now beginning. Ask God for signs, wonders,
and miracles that will intervene in old cyclical structures of
your life. Be secure in timing. Declare that everything in
your past be repaired and restored so that your future can
be unlocked. Look up and see the window of heaven that is
opening over you.[36]

God's Timing

Ask Yourself

Do you know that there is a Creator who transcends and enters time to commune with His children so they may efficiently walk in time?

When the generations begin to prophesy and speak forth the same thing, then you see heaven, the earth, and the future realigned.

Remember

Call to Me and I will answer you and show you great and mighty things, fenced in and hidden, which you do not know (do not distinguish and recognize, have knowledge of and understand).

—JEREMIAH 33:3, AMP

Man's Timing

Ask Yourself

Are you praying for God to reveal Himself to you in an unusual way? Ask Him to come and commune with you today.

Revelation comes in a moment in time. How you commit to revelation is how the power and force of what was revealed manifest.

Remember

Do not be conformed to this world, but be transformed by the renewing of your mind, that you may prove what is that good and acceptable and perfect will of God.

—ROMANS 12:2

Heavenly Angels

*Understanding that there are two angels for every
demon—faithful allies who are battle-tested and proven
in the timeless ages of the past*

LIFE EXISTS IN other dimensions beyond the earth! There are other beings from another dimension that are moving by the multitudes across the vast expanse of our known world. These beings are not subject to the limitations of our world. Beyond our normal range of understanding is another dimension more real and lasting than any we could imagine. In this realm exist these living beings called angels, along with their dark cousins, demons. Created by God, these timeless beings have a history of their own. Remarkably, they have the ability to come and go between the eternal dimension and our world.

There are realms of reality and life beyond human reach and reason without supernatural assistance. The angels, God's hosts, are among such mysteries. Yes, these supernatural beings are found throughout the Scriptures, from the first page to the last page of the Bible.[37]

Fallen Angels

Comprehending that Satan and the fallen angels desire to
dominate the worship of the people of God

EZEKIEL 28 TAKES us back, beyond our history, to a land of Eden prior to the garden. Lucifer is described as "the seal of perfection, full of wisdom and perfect in beauty" (v. 12). While still perfect, he ruled over a land called Eden. "You were in Eden, the garden of God" (v. 13). In that garden, this angel king was covered in great wealth and also surrounded by a vast amount of musical instruments.

Lucifer was anointed for high purpose, yet Lucifer committed iniquity even though he was created perfect. Lucifer began to crave the worship for himself! God cast Lucifer out of his leadership role. When he fell, the old earth was destroyed as if an asteroid had hit! All life was abolished, and the earth became without form and void. In that rebellion one-third of the angelic hosts fell with him.

Lucifer became Satan, the archenemy of God and His purpose for man.[38]

Heavenly Angels

Ask Yourself

Did you know that angels are assigned the responsibility to serve believers?

The hosts of heaven were brought to life by the Creator God. They were given a deathless, timeless existence very different from the history of humans.

Remember

You alone are the LORD; You have made heaven, the heaven of heavens, with all their host, the earth and everything on it...and You preserve them all. The host of heaven worships You.

—NEHEMIAH 9:6

Fallen Angels

Ask Yourself

Are you aware that Satan and his fallen angels—known as demons—live to thwart Christians from fulfilling their purpose?

Satan desires the Creator's position, preeminence, people, and power. He wants to sit on "the mount of the congregation."

Remember

You were perfect in your ways from the day you were created, till iniquity was found in you....Therefore I cast you...out of the mountain of God; and I destroyed you.

—EZEKIEL 28:15–16

The Battlefield of the Mind

*Beginning deliverance by first removing that which
defends the enemy*

THE MOST PRECIOUS commodity in the earth realm is the mind. Not only is God vying for your minds, but the enemy is vying for your minds as well. Revelation 18:11–16 states that in the last days, the intellectual property of the soul will be one of the commodities bought and sold in the marketplace and used to drive entire economies.

Achieving victory over the enemy requires discipline. To get this discipline, the first thing is to know what thoughts qualify to legitimately be in your mind. Philippians 4:8 says, "Finally, brethren, whatsoever things are true, whatsoever things are honest, whatsoever things are just, whatsoever things are pure, whatsoever things are lovely, whatsoever things are of good report; if there be any virtue, and if there be any praise, think on these things" (KJV). If your thoughts are not true, honest, just, pure, lovely, of good report, or praiseworthy, do not allow those thoughts to take root in your mind.[39]

Your Enemy Opponent

*Prevailing and overcoming against every attack
of the enemy*

THERE ARE TWO kingdoms mentioned in the Bible. The line on the battlefield has been drawn between the kingdom of darkness and the kingdom of light. Every individual must choose one side or the other. As believers, thank God we have been delivered from the authorities that rule in the kingdom of darkness. God has ordained that even as Christ is the head of the church and the church is His body, we are assured of victory over every demonic force in Jesus's name.

Although the Bible makes it clear that we have won the victory over Satan and his evil kingdom through Christ, there is still a war waging for our souls. Therefore we must be aware of who this enemy is and how he operates. The kingdom of darkness is well equipped and very ready to fight a pitched battle using any and all means at its disposal. Like all good generals, it is to your benefit to be well aware of the inner workings of the enemy.[40]

The Battlefield of the Mind

Ask Yourself

Are you actively asking God to remove mind-sets, thought patterns, and processes that cause you to act, react, and respond contrary to the ways of God and a godly lifestyle?

Through deliberate ingestions of God's Word, the strongholds of the enemy can be forced out and the things of God can come in and occupy our thought life.

Remember

The word of God is living and active and sharper than any two-edged sword, and...able to judge the thoughts and intentions of the heart.

—HEBREWS 4:12, NAS

Your Enemy Opponent

Ask Yourself

Can you answer these questions: Who is the enemy? Where is the battle? What are your weapons?

As the enemy wages war against you, remember that you are fighting the good fight of faith. The weapons you fight with are powerful and operate at their peak in the spirit realm.

Remember

Gird up the loins of your mind....[Be] ye stedfast, unmoveable, always abounding in the work of the Lord, forasmuch as ye know that your labour is not in vain in the Lord.

—1 PETER 1:13; 1 CORINTHIANS 15:58, KJV

Alone

Feeling completely happy and satisfied in your own heart and life

THE WORD ALONE emphasizes more of a physical sense than the emotional involvement implied by the word *lonely*. When one is *solitary* (alone), it may indicate isolation as a chosen course. In essence, being *alone* does not necessarily make one *lonely*, and being *lonely* does not necessarily come because one is *alone*. Being alone is primarily a physical reality; loneliness is a state of mind.

Thank God that we have a High Priest who can sympathize with our times of loneliness. All of Jesus's disciples and friends abandoned Him in the hours before He faced the cross. But Jesus had these words to say about that time: "Behold, the hour cometh, yea, is now come, that ye shall be scattered, every man to his own, and shall leave me alone: and yet I am not alone, because the Father is with me" (John 16:32, KJV).

We are never alone, and there is no need to feel lonely, because God is with us![41]

Loneliness

Being without company, desolate, and longing for companionship

L ONELINESS IS DEFINED as "the state of being lonely, being without company, desolate, producing a feeling of bleakness or desolation." The word *lonely* implies a longing for companionship. Loneliness becomes a fatal distraction when it leads to sadness, dejection, and a sense of desolation that cause you to lose sight of the promise made by Jesus: "I will never leave thee, nor forsake thee" (Heb. 13:5).

The distraction of loneliness causes an echo in the soul, a reverberation of thoughts and questions that bounce around in your spirit, ultimately springing from a sense of emptiness. *Does anybody see me? Does anybody know what I'm going through? Does anybody understand? Does anybody really care?*

Lonely heart, allow the loving hand of God to reach down into your mind, heart, and spirit and drive out the feelings of isolation and disconnection that plague you. Open your eyes and see, really see, where you are and what you have as a child of God.[42]

Alone

Ask Yourself

Have you elevated your mind above your circumstances and realized that a true sense of connection and complete-ness can only come from within you?

Embrace the will and plan of God for your life, and let your wholeness come from Him in whom there is no lack, only inexhaustible supply.

Remember

I will never leave thee, nor forsake thee.
—HEBREWS 13:5, KJV

Loneliness

Ask Yourself

Have you attempted to cover up your loneliness by throwing yourself into the hustle and bustle of life instead of dealing with the root cause for your loneliness?

Stop seeking fulfillment and identity from external sources, especially from other people, and denounce the fatal distraction of loneliness.

Remember

Turn to me and be gracious to me, for I am lonely and afflicted.

—PSALM 25:16, NIV

Answered Prayer

Believing that you will have what you ask for in prayer

W HAT ARE THE basics of effective prayer? Are there other elements we need—other *mechanisms* that are important to ensure that every prayer is effective? Yes. The Bible has a great deal to say about prayer. Philippians 4:6 is rich with information and instruction about prayer.

Paul says, "Let your requests be made known to God." Doesn't God know everything? Yes, He does. And He knows your requests before you ask them. The purpose of making the requests for your needs is not for God's benefit—but for yours.

Paul also admonishes: "Be anxious for nothing." Nothing…everything. There is nothing left out of everything. And Paul puts a *condition* on these requests, namely that you pray in "supplication, with thanksgiving." So when you bring your requests before God in prayer "and supplication," it means to recognize your place. God is God, and you are His child. Don't get the two mixed up![43]

Unanswered Prayer

Misunderstanding that you must ask the right way for your prayers to be answered

THROUGH JESUS, WE have been given *permission* (or authority) to expect answered prayer and the *ability* to conduct God's operations in this world, but if you stand there asking for the ability when you already have it, you are essentially calling God a liar. He has said you have it; you are saying you don't. This is the point: God has a proper order for us to follow, and things will not work unless we do it His way.

Moreover, you cannot *make* God do anything. Do you really think that by nagging the Creator of the universe you can browbeat Him into doing something He doesn't really want to do? If God is eternal, can your repeated crabbing—even if you do it ten times a day, every day of your life—influence a Being who has been around since before time began? Do you think God can't outlast you?

As long as you ask in line with what God has said, it will be given you.[44]

Answered Prayer

Ask Yourself

Have you made your requests—*all your requests, big and small*—known to God?

Some people think supplication means groveling, but a working definition of supplication is simply "a prayer for God's help, or to humbly ask."

Remember

Be anxious for nothing, but in everything by prayer and supplication, with thanksgiving, let your requests be made known to God.

—PHILIPPIANS 4:6

Unanswered Prayer

Ask Yourself

Are you asking God for something that will lead you into sin? God cannot sin, and therefore He will not participate in your sin.

God's grace and His promises are available to everyone.
He is an equal opportunity blesser!

Remember

Ask, and it will be given to you; seek, and you will find; knock, and it will be opened to you. For everyone who asks receives…he who seeks finds…to him who knocks it will be opened.
—LUKE 11:9–10

What Love Is

Loving like Christ

SAINT PAUL WRITES, "Though I speak with the tongues of men and of angels…" (1 Cor. 13:1). What if I was eloquent in every language on the earth? What if I was eloquent in every dialect on the planet? It would be a human instinct to say, "I am something." But, through the pen of Paul, God says, "Without love, you are nothing."

So often, these are the qualifiers of our love: We love others because they love us first. We love others because they come up to our expectations. Or we love others because they are made of the *right stuff*! But Christ has no qualifiers on His love. Christ loved us "while we were yet sinners" (Rom. 5:8, KJV). He loved us when we were covered with the stench of sin. He loved us unconditionally.

Without love, you have no value. The Bible describes the complexity and majesty of God with these three words: "God is love" (1 John 4:16). Christ gave His love when it was not deserved to people who did not deserve it. We must learn to do the same.[45]

What Love Is Not

Mistaking your emotions for love

LOVE IS NOT an emotion. Jesus didn't say, "I was hungry, and you felt sorry for Me." No! He said, "I was hungry and you gave Me no food; I was thirsty and you gave Me no drink; I was a stranger and you did not take Me in, naked and you did not clothe Me, sick and in prison and you did not visit Me" (Matt. 25:42–43).

Love is not what you feel. Love is what you do. *Works*…not words…are proof of your love.

Love is not sex.

Love is not the urge to merge.

There is "free love" and "covenant love." And you better know the difference. Free love takes, and covenant love gives. Free love will give you AIDS and a home in the lake of fire. Covenant love gives you a ring and makes your life as the days of heaven on earth. Your choices have consequences. In 1 Corinthians 13:5, Paul says that love is not self-seeking. Remember that love does not insist on its own way. Love does not pursue a selfish advantage.

Love looks for a way to give![46]

What Love Is

Ask Yourself

Are you loving others the way Christ loves you? Jesus commanded us to "love one another as I have loved you" (John 15:12).

Unless we love, we are not the sons and daughters of God, no matter what church membership we claim or spiritual experience we profess.

Remember

He who does not love does not know God, for God is love.

—1 JOHN 4:8

What Love Is Not

Ask Yourself

Do you personify the characteristics of love found in Ruth 1:16–17?

A bell is not a bell until you ring it. A song is not a song until you sing it. Love in your heart is not put there to stay. Love is not love until you give it away.[47]

Remember

Entreat me not to leave you…for wherever you go, I will go…your people shall be my people, and your God, my God. Where you die, I will die, and there will I be buried.

—RUTH 1:16–17

The Fear of God

Reverencing God anew in your daily walk and life

A PERSON WHO FEARS God trembles at His Word and in His presence (Isa. 66:2; Jer. 5:22). What does it mean to tremble at His Word? It can all be summed up in one statement: to willingly obey God even when it appears more advantageous to compromise or not obey His Word.

Our hearts must be firmly established in the fact that God is good. He is not a child abuser. A person who fears God knows this, for he knows God's character. That is why he or she will draw near to God even when others would draw back in terror.

That person realizes that any immediate or impending difficulty encountered at God's hand will ultimately bring forth good in the end. It is in times of hardship that what we *truly believe* is clearly revealed. Only then will our faith be seen for what it is by the light of the fire of trials.

The fear of the Lord will keep us from compromising God's truth for the pursuit of personal gain.[48]

Afraid of God

Trembling or drawing back from the presence of the glory of God

WHEN ISRAEL LEFT Egypt, Moses led the people to Mount Sinai, where God would reveal His glory. When God began to reveal His glory, "there were thunderings and lightnings, and a thick cloud on the mountain; and the sound of the trumpet was very loud, so that all the people who were in the camp trembled" (Exod. 19:16).

Notice that the people trembled and drew back. They no longer wanted to hear God's audible voice. Neither did they want to look upon or be in the presence of His glory—they were unable to bear it.

Moses said, "Do not fear." Then he said that God had come "...that His fear may be before you" (Exod. 20:20). This verse makes a distinction between *being afraid of God* and *fearing Him*. Moses feared God, but the people did not. "So the people stood afar off, but Moses drew near the thick darkness where God was" (v. 21). Israel drew back, but Moses drew near.

Are you drawing back from God, or are you drawing near to Him?[49]

The Fear of God

Ask Yourself

Are you willing to obey God even when it appears more advantageous to compromise or not obey His Word?

To fear God is to believe God. To believe God is to obey Him.

Remember

The secret of the LORD is with those who fear Him.

—PSALM 25:14

Afraid of God

Ask Yourself

Do you get God's Word from your pastor but withdraw from the mountain of God? Are you afraid to hear His voice, which lays bare the condition of your heart?

The fear of God is our only protection from hypocrisy. Then we will not hide sin in our heart, because we will fear God more than the opinions of mortal men. We will turn our hearts to the Lord!

Remember

The LORD is a friend to those who fear him. He teaches them his covenant.

—PSALM 25:14, NLT

Fasting for Breakthrough

Refraining from food for a spiritual purpose

FASTING HAS ALWAYS been a normal part of a relationship with God. As expressed by the impassioned plea of David in Psalm 42, fasting brings one into a deeper, more intimate, and more powerful relationship with the Lord.

When you eliminate food from your diet for a number of days, your spirit becomes uncluttered by the things of this world and amazingly sensitive to the things of God. As David stated, "Deep calls unto deep" (Ps. 42:7). David was fasting. His hunger and thirst for God were greater than his natural desire for food. As a result, he reached a place where he could cry out from the depths of his spirit to the depths of God, even in the midst of his trial. Once you've experienced even a glimpse of that kind of intimacy with our God—our Father, the holy Creator of the universe—and the countless rewards and blessings that follow, your whole perspective will change. You will soon realize that fasting is a secret source of power that is overlooked by many.[50]

King Stomach's Reign

*Allowing King Stomach to rule your appetite and
control your life*

IT HAS BEEN said that the way to a man's heart is through
his stomach. Consider for just a moment what has happened
to the human race under the rule of King Stomach.

In the Garden of Eden, the serpent was cunning and
convinced Eve that she should eat from the forbidden tree.
With that one meal Adam and Eve immediately went from
peacefully enjoying God's presence in the cool of the garden
to fearfully hiding from His presence among the trees of
the garden.

King Stomach was high and lifted up in Esau, the son of
Isaac and Rebekah. When Esau returned from the field one
day, he was hungry. His brother, Jacob, was about to have a
simple meal of red lentils and bread, so Esau begged Jacob
for the same meal. Esau sold his coveted birthright because
of his allegiance to King Stomach.

The children of Israel murmured and complained until
God gave them quail to eat—and they ate themselves right
out of the Promised Land.[51]

Fasting for Breakthrough

Ask Yourself

Do you desire to know God's will for your life…whom you should marry…or what to do in a critical situation? Are you willing to fast for your breakthrough?

The three duties of every Christian are giving, praying, and fasting. When you faithfully follow these three duties, God rewards you openly.

Remember

As the deer pants for the water brooks, so pants my soul for You, O God! My soul thirsts for God, for the living God.

—PSALM 42:1–2

King Stomach's Reign

Ask Yourself

Have you realized how crucially important it is to dethrone King Stomach from your life through a spiritual fast?

You will have to choose to dethrone that "dictator within."

Remember

> Then Jesus…was led by the Spirit into the wilderness, being tempted for forty days by the devil. And in those days He ate nothing, and afterward…He was hungry.
>
> —LUKE 4:1–2

Rebuilt by the Holy Spirit

Letting the Holy Spirit restore you to the person you were meant to be

THERE IS A genuine possibility of personal restoration and fulfillment for everyone, regardless of what your past may hold, but that personal restoration can only occur at the invitation of the Holy Spirit and under His ongoing tutelage.

We have all experienced something of brokenness: hearts, homes, health, finance, dreams, relationships—all as breakable as bones, though harder to set. We may not all be basket cases, but it's certain we all need the Doctor.

The Doctor is God, who is larger than any brokenness and is the fountainhead of life itself. He is the Father of love, and He has the right to speak with authority to His children. He has given us His Word, and He enlivens it to our human hearts. The Holy Spirit has come to glorify Jesus, the Son of God. Jesus is glorified most of all through our human personalities. The Father created us in splendor, in His own image, but the splendor has been badly marred. Jesus came to redeem the Father's original intention in us and through us.[52]

Broken-Down Walls of Sin

*Trying to face the enemy without the protection of your
spiritual walls of defense*

YOUR SALVATION SOLVES the problem of your relationship with God, but it doesn't always dissolve the problems
in your life. It opens the doorway to solutions, but it is only by
walking through that door and patiently pursuing that way
that those problems will finally be resolved.

This fact stands out so clearly in the Book of Nehemiah.
Here is the story of a people who had been given a new lease
on life but who were repeatedly embarrassed by their inability
to demonstrate complete evidence of renewal. Nehemiah
came from a distant land to begin—and to complete—the
rebuilding process by which the walls of Jerusalem would be
restored from the rubble of past destruction.

Nehemiah, a handbook for personal restoration, shows
how the Holy Spirit assists us in rebuilding our brokenness,
strengthening our weaknesses, and leading us into victory.

We need more than rebirth—we need rebuilding as well.
Our Savior has sent His Holy Spirit to partner with us in
the rebuilding of every part of our lives.[53]

Rebuilt by the Holy Spirit

Ask Yourself

Have you heard God's voice saying, "Come, return to Me; come back"? Are you ready to allow the Holy Spirit to rebuild your life?

He who has come to help you see your life rebuilt will also come to see your life advanced into His purposes. He will respond to your every prayer, and He will nurture your soul, reminding you of His loving character and His clear truth.

Remember

Now may the God of peace Himself sanctify you completely; and may your whole spirit, soul, and body be preserved blameless at the coming of our Lord Jesus Christ.

—1 THESSALONIANS 5:23

Broken-Down Walls of Sin

Ask Yourself

Do you feel overwhelmed by the circumstances of life? Have you asked God to show you what He's doing?

The Holy Spirit, your Nehemiah, will restore, establish, strengthen, and settle you, today and every day of the rest of your life.

Remember

Do not despise the chastening of the LORD, nor detest His correction; for whom the LORD loves He corrects, just as a father the son in whom he delights.

—PROVERBS 3:11–12

Facing Tomorrow With Joy

Trusting your future to God's Holy Spirit

BREATHE DEEPLY. Do it again, please. Now touch the most solid object near you and answer this question: Which of these two is the most important to sustaining your life—breath or material things?

Simple to answer, isn't it? Breath, of course. Without breathing we cannot live. It's the same with the breath of God's Spirit, infused with His Word, which together are the source and sustaining power of our spiritual lives.

Dear friend, I want to send you into all your tomorrows with the Word of God in your hand and the joy of the Lord in your heart. The Word that created all worlds is the Word that is completing you. Rest in that assurance, and rejoice in His Word as He "rebuilds the real you," the "you" He intended when He created you.

And don't miss recognizing the helper here today in your life: the Holy Spirit. The Holy Spirit is ready now to take you from this moment onward toward the fulfillment of Father God's high destiny for you.[54]

Facing Tomorrow With Fear

Missing out on the Holy Spirit's work in your life

WHEN NEHEMIAH RECEIVED a report that the Israelites who had returned to Jerusalem were in great distress and reproach, he asked: "What is the cause of their problem?" The answer: "The wall of Jerusalem is broken down and its gates are burned."

This answer focused on the embarrassment of a people whose relationship with God had been restored, yet the people recognized the incompleteness of their situation. In short, they had a life with God but had no evidence of it affecting their daily details of life.

Have you ever sensed this dilemma yourself? Are you born again, yet parts of your personality are a contradiction to the power of the God you worship? After evaluating your life and noting how much is broken down and "burned with fire," you may feel the same sense of reproach and distress the returning exiles felt.

If you do, take hope. Let the Holy Spirit restore you to the person you were meant to be!55

Facing Tomorrow With Joy

Ask Yourself

What is most important to you—the breath of God's Spirit or the feel of your material possessions?

The Holy Spirit wants to bring you to the full realization of God's purposes, patterns, and promises for your life.

Remember

In Your presence is fullness of joy; at Your right hand are pleasures forevermore.

—PSALM 16:11

Facing Tomorrow With Fear

Ask Yourself

Why am I so shaken by fears? Why can't I defend myself against temptation? Why do I always feel so worthless?

Wherever your walls were destroyed and you were destitute, God will establish you and make you secure by the power of His love.

Remember

May the God of all grace, who called us to His eternal glory by Christ Jesus, after you have suffered a while, perfect, establish, strengthen, and settle you.

—1 PETER 5:10

NOTES

1. Adapted from Matthew Hagee, *Shaken, Not Shattered* (Lake Mary, FL: Charisma House, 2009), 1.

2. Adapted from Jack Hayford, *Rebuilding the Real You* (Lake Mary, FL: Charisma House, 2009), 208.

3. Ibid.

4. R. T. Kendall, *Total Forgiveness* (Lake Mary, FL: Charisma House, 2002, 2007).

5. Ibid.

6. Jentezen Franklin, *Fear Fighters* (Lake Mary, FL: Charisma House, 2009).

7. Harvey Mackay, "Worrying Makes You Cross the Bridge Before You Come to It," HarveyMackey.com, http://www.harveymackay.com/columns/best/13.cfm (accessed January 19, 2010).

8. Franklin, *Fear Fighters*.

9. John Hagee, *Life's Challenges—Your Opportunities* (Lake Mary, FL: Charisma House, 2009).

10. Ibid.

11. Don Dickerman, *When Pigs Move In* (Lake Mary, FL: Charisma House, 2009).

12. Ibid.

13. Francis Frangipane, *When Many Are One* (Lake Mary, FL: Charisma House, 2009).

14. Ibid.

15. John Eckhardt, *God Still Speaks* (Lake Mary, FL: Charisma House, 2009).

16. R. T. Kendall, *Controlling the Tongue* (Lake Mary, FL: Charisma House, 2007).

17. John Bevere, *The Bait of Satan* (Lake Mary, FL: Charisma House, 1997, 2007).

18. Ibid.

19. Bill Wiese, *23 Minutes in Hell* (Lake Mary, FL: Charisma House, 2006).

20. Ibid.

21. Perry Stone, *The Meal That Heals* (Lake Mary, FL: Charisma House, 2008).

22. Ibid.

23. Francis Frangipane, *The Shelter of the Most High* (Lake Mary, FL: Charisma House, 2008).

24. Ibid.

25. Hank Kunneman, *The Revealer of Secrets* (Lake Mary, FL: Charisma House, 2009).

26. Ibid.

27. Kimberly Daniels, *Give It Back!* (Lake Mary, FL: Charisma House, 2007).

28. Ibid.

29. Joseph Prince, *Unmerited Favor* (Lake Mary, FL: Charisma House, 2010).

30. Ibid.

31. Ibid.

32. Ibid.

33. Joyce Meyer, *Conflict-Free Living* (Lake Mary, FL: Charisma House, 2008).

34. Ibid.

35. Chuck Pierce, *Interpreting the Times* (Lake Mary, FL: Charisma House, 2008).

36. Ibid.

37. Ron Phillips, *Our Invisible Allies* (Lake Mary, FL: Charisma House, 2009).

38. Ibid.

39. Cindy Trimm, *The Rules of Engagement* (Lake Mary, FL: Charisma House, 2008).

40. Ibid.

41. Joyce L. Rodgers, *Fatal Distractions* (Lake Mary, FL: Charisma House, 2003).

42. Ibid.

43. Frederick K. C. Price, *Answered Prayer—Guaranteed* (Lake Mary, FL: Charisma House, 2006).

44. Ibid.

45. John and Diana Hagee, *What Every Man Wants in a Woman, What Every Woman Wants in a Man* (Lake Mary, FL: Charisma House, 2005).

46. Ibid.

47. This quote is attributed to Oscar Hammerstein II, who gave it as advice to Mary Martin.

48. John Bevere, *The Fear of the Lord* (Lake Mary, FL: Charisma House, 1997, 2006).

49. Ibid.

50. Jentezen Franklin, *Fasting* (Lake Mary, FL: Charisma House, 2008).

51. Ibid.

52. Hayford, *Rebuilding the Real You*.

53. Ibid.

54. Ibid.

55. Ibid.

Journal Pages

_____

_____

_____

_____

_____

_____

_____

_____

_____

_____

_____

_____

_____

_____

_____

_____

_____

_____

_____

_____

_____

_____

_____

_____

_____

_____

_____

_____

_____

_____

_____

_____

_____

_____